JOYCE SIDMAN is the author of *The Girl who Drew Butterflies* (Houghton Mifflin Harcourt), which received the Sibert Medal, as well as *Dark Emperor and Other Poems of the Night* (Houghton Mifflin Harcourt), a Newbery Honor Book. Her other books include *Swirl by Swirl*, *Winter Bees*, and *Before Morning* (all Houghton Mifflin Harcourt). For her acclaimed body of work, she has received the NCTE Award for Excellence in Poetry for Children. When she's not writing, Joyce enjoys exploring the woods near her home in Wayzata, Minnesota. Visit Joyce's website at joycesidman.com.

MIREN ASIAIN LORA is the illustrator of *A Good Day* (Eerdmans). She lives in Spain, where she studied fine arts at the University of the Basque Country. Her artwork has been shown in exhibitions in several different countries. In her illustrations, Miren works to convey the magic of everyday life. Visit Miren's website at miaslo.com.

For Clara, Earth Warrior, who has opened my eyes.
—J. S.

To Mati, partner in all of my wanderings.
—M. A. L.

Joyce Sidman would like to thank National Geographic Certified Educator Jill Holz and her Earth Science class at Wayzata High School for helping her with the intricacies of how Earth works.

First published in the United States in 2021
by Eerdmans Books for Young Readers,
an imprint of Wm. B. Eerdmans Publishing Co.
Grand Rapids, Michigan
Text © 2021 Joyce Sidman

www.eerdmans.com/youngreaders

Illustrations first published in Spain in 2016 in *Versos de la Tierra*
by Ediciones SM, Madrid
© 2016 Ediciones SM
Illustrations © 2016 Miren Asiain Lora

Manufactured in China.

29 28 27 26 25 24 23 22   3 4 5 6 7 8 9

ISBN 978-0-8028-5528-2

A catalog record of this book is available from the Library of Congress.

Illustrations created with watercolor and acrylic.

Written by
JOYCE SIDMAN

Illustrated by
MIREN ASIAIN LORA

HELLO, EARTH!

POEMS TO OUR PLANET

EERDMANS BOOKS FOR YOUNG READERS

GRAND RAPIDS, MICHIGAN

HELLO, EARTH!

It's your children.
Some of your children—
the human ones.
We have been studying you, Earth,
but we long to learn more.

We want to ask you
a few questions.
We want to
tell you our dreams
and wishes.

Can you hear us,
Earth?

7

FLOATING

Earth,
we've seen pictures of you
floating in space,
circling the sun with your
brothers and sisters.

From far away
you look so perfect.

But Earth . . .

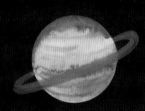

. . . we are standing
right on top of you!

How can we be
here,
climbing trees, walking paths,
staring up at constellations . . .

and also out
in deepest space?

Does that mean
that each of us
is floating
among the stars?

BIG AND SMALL

Earth,
it's hard to imagine
just how big you are.
Bigger than a mountain,
or the sky,
or anything we
have seen, or felt, or touched.

Earth,
how can we ever understand
your bigness?
Our smallness?

We need to figure out
the way
we fit together.

LONG MEMORY

You were so different once:
a huge spinning cloud of gas,
a vast swirling sea of lava.
Finally your crust cooled
and settled into land

and water.

Even then, you kept changing.
You've felt giant footsteps

trample your back,
ancient roots dig into your soil,
fantastical leaves and flowers
breathe your air.

Earth,
you must have a very long memory.
Which was your favorite part?

FIERY

Deep inside
your core,
you still have a fiery heart.

Sometimes your hot insides
squeeze up
through hidden cracks
and explode!

How does it feel,
Earth,
to have parts of you
erupt like a new tooth?

A tooth as big
as a mountain:
a glow,

a flow . . .

a VOLCANO!

EARTH QUAKES

Your crust is always
shifting. Slowly,
over millions of years,
huge parts of you
wrinkle and ripple.
They slide over and under,
pull apart,
and smoosh together.

Do we see this happen? No.
It's too slow.

But sometimes
we feel it.
When you're extra excited,
you lose your rocky grip
and slip.
We feel a jolt, a blip, a tremble.

Earth,
we feel you
quake.

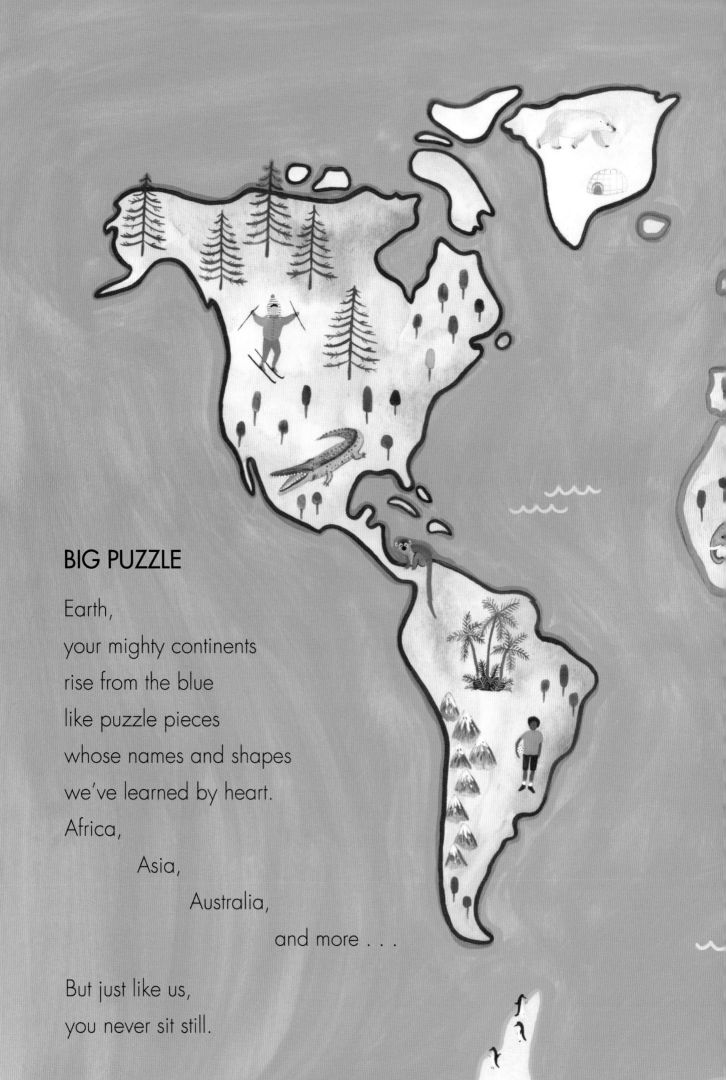

BIG PUZZLE

Earth,
your mighty continents
rise from the blue
like puzzle pieces
whose names and shapes
we've learned by heart.
Africa,
     Asia,
          Australia,
               and more . . .

But just like us,
you never sit still.

Inch by inch,
your continents creep,
your oceans widen.

You become a new puzzle,
every day.

SUNLIGHT, MOONLIGHT

What is it like
to spin

and feel the sun
warm all your
beautiful places,
        one by one?

What is it like
to feel
the cool sweep
of the moon?

One so close,
a silver sister.

One so far,
a burning star.

EXPLORERS

Every morning,
the sun
opens our eyes,
sends us out of doors
to explore you.

Sun unlocks
your scent, your color,
your promise.

Every morning feels
fresh:
a new gift
we can't wait
        to open.

JUNGLE

At your
bulging equator,
green
sprouts from
every nook and cranny.

Roots sink deep
        to drink in water.
Leaves spread wide
        to capture sunlight.

Out of this,
plants make food and air
for us, whether we walk,
fly, slither, or perch.

We live and breathe
because plants
        live and breathe.

How clever of you,
Earth.

MOUNTAINS

In your craggy

places

where rocks jut high,

the air

is crisp as ice.

Trees bristle with needles.

Snow

floats down

in feathery flakes,

gathers in crunchy layers,

and stays

    and stays

        and stays.

Earth, are you
saving all that
frozen water for a time
you'll really need it?

DESERT

Even in heat,
even in blasted sand,
even in dry bones,
you sparkle with life.

Do you ever feel burnt
or scratchy?
Or do you welcome
the wind
that sends each
grain of sand skittering?

Earth,
do you love your dry places
as much as your
watery ones?
Your tropics
as much as your ice?

TIDES

Where pools of salty water
meet fingers of rock,
the tide slowly
        swells and rises,
ebbs and sinks.
Twice a day,
        every day.

Earth, is it true
that the moon
pulls at your oceans
with her twirling gravity?

Your waves surge toward her
when she's near,
then fall back as she passes?

Is it like a dance?
Do you need each other
for balance,
just as we do?

WATER PLANET

Earth,
so much
of your surface
is water!

We like to imagine
floating across your seas
on our own private island.

But the ocean does not belong to us.
It is home to those
who dive and dart and billow,
whose fins flash,

whose branches
gently sift out what they need.

Creatures whose bodies
breathe water
instead of air.

GIANTS

And the sea belongs
to giants
who roll and spout
and rise
like wet, streaming mountains.
Their tails tower
far above us.

How small
we feel beside them,
yet our hearts grow
large
and light.

DEEP CURRENTS

Long ago
we came from
the sea,
and it calls to us.

Plunge down to deep worlds,
it says.
Follow bright, flickering fish
and swirls of tiny plankton;
feel cool currents
brush your skin
and lift your hair.

Earth,
we feel those currents
pump inside us.
Maybe we are
water creatures,
too.

NOISY

Do we ever bother you
with our noise, Earth?
With our digging
and building
and shouting
and grabbing
and rushing around
making messes?

We want
    so much
for ourselves,
Earth.

We forget to be happy
with what
you have already
given us.

OUR PART

Earth,

we are part of you.

We are connected.

In taking care of you,

we take care of ourselves.

Help us remember

the quiet, daily things

we can do

to keep your water clean,
your air fresh,
your soil full of life.
To reuse what we already have
and leave room for
wild things.

Do you think we can do it,
Earth?
Can we work as hard
    for you
as we do for ourselves?

QUESTIONS AND ANSWERS

Earth,

we know that you

can't answer all our questions

in words.

You answer in other ways:

a crackling thunderstorm

that shows us how each

precious drop of water

cycles up

    and down,

over and

    over again . . .

. . . or a mighty wind
that scares us
a little
(okay, a lot!)
and reminds us
we are not in charge.

Sometimes

you answer us gently

with the lapping of waves,

slow and steady like

the beat

of our hearts.

Maybe your answers
are just
      what we need
to make us
   stop
      and look
         and think
about how
wondrous you are.

MYSTERIES

We hope you
still have secret places,
Earth:
hidden forces,
mysterious plants
and creatures . . .

undiscovered,
    unexplained.

We hope
you will always be
one step
ahead of us.

RAINBOW

Earth,
we have studied you
and seen ourselves:
so varied, so much the same.
Changing, growing,
learning
how to be together.
The oxygen from your plants
breathes through us.
The water from your depths
flows inside of us.
You are all we need.

We love you, Earth.

MORE ABOUT HOW THE EARTH WORKS

EARTH'S AGE

(Hello, Earth!)

Earth as a planet is 4.55 billion years old, but life developed very slowly, over millions and millions (and millions!) of years. Humans (*Homo sapiens*) evolved just in the last two hundred thousand years—and we have been trying to understand how Earth works ever since.

EARTH'S SIZE

(Floating, Big and Small)

Earth is so big that no one had ever seen it whole until astronauts journeyed into space in the late 1960s and took photographs from their spaceships. For the first time, we saw our planet as a beautiful blue and green sphere, floating in black space.

EARTH'S HISTORY

(Long Memory)

Earth has changed so much since it came into being. It was fiery hot at first—part gas, part molten material. When it began to cool, huge clouds of water vapor formed, which rained and rained for millions of years, creating our oceans. Life developed underwater and spread to the land. As Earth's surface changed, all sorts of plants and animals evolved and then became extinct. How do we know? We have found their fossils.

EARTH'S LAYERS

(Fiery)

In its present state, our planet is like a giant ball with many layers. The deeper you go, the hotter it gets, and the more pressure builds up. The center of Earth is called the core, made up of a super-dense iron ball surrounded by molten metal. Around the core is a thick layer called the mantle, which is solid but can also move very slowly, like Silly Putty. At the surface of Earth (where we live) is a very thin, cooler layer called the crust. Sometimes "hot spots" form in the crust, where bits of mantle melt and push upwards, causing volcanoes. Other volcanoes form when sections of crust collide with each other (see "Plate Tectonics" below).

PLATE TECTONICS

(Earth Quakes)

Although it's hard to tell by looking, Earth's layers are always moving and shifting, because heat constantly rises from the core toward the crust. The big chunks of land above the ocean—what we call continents— are riding on huge "plates" of crust that move very, very slowly (at about the same rate your fingernails grow). According to a scientific theory called plate tectonics, these plates crash and slide against each other. Sometimes, when moving, the plates snag on each other and pressure builds up below the surface. When they finally break free, we feel the Earth quake.

CONTINENTAL DRIFT

(Big Puzzle)

Because of this constant movement, Earth's continents have drifted and changed shape over time. In the past, all land on Earth was one huge continent. Gradually, that landmass broke up and spread apart. Our continents are still moving. Scientists predict that in 250 million years, all of today's continents will have drifted back together again!

ROTATION AND ORBIT

(Sun and Moon, Explorers)

Our whole sense of time—and the structure of our lives—is based on the movement of the Earth and the moon.

For thousands of years, humans have marked a new day with the arrival of the sun each morning. Eventually, astronomers discovered that Earth itself is spinning on its axis, and one full rotation equals a day. We see the sun again because the Earth has rotated completely to face the sun once more.

Likewise, a month was considered the period between full moons. We have learned that this is the time it takes the moon to orbit around the Earth. When we see a full moon, we know that the moon is back at the same position in its orbit that it was a month ago.

Earth, as it spins, also orbits around the sun (which is much bigger than Earth and has stronger gravity). Seasons change during this long orbit because Earth's axis is tilted, so different parts of the planet receive more sunlight at different times. The period between one spring and the next is what we call a year: the time it takes Earth to complete one orbit around the sun.

POWERHOUSE PLANTS

(Jungle)

Three basic things are essential to our life on Earth: sun, water, and plants. The sun is the source of all light and energy. Water cycles through our world, regulating Earth's temperature and carrying important chemicals and nutrients to every living thing. But plants are the quiet powerhouses of Earth. They absorb sunlight, water, and carbon dioxide, and use them to create food—for themselves and all creatures on Earth. Their leaves, fruits, and roots feed us and other animals. As plants grow, they also give off oxygen, which we need to breathe. Without plants, animals could not exist. Thank you, plants!

ALTITUDE

(Mountains)

Earth's surface is not smooth; it is bunched and wrinkled. Some parts are high, and some low. The weather changes at different altitudes (or heights). In very high places, such as mountaintops, the air stays cooler and windier than down below. On many mountaintops, snow falls for most of the year, building up into thick rivers of ice called glaciers. Glaciers store large amounts of fresh water, providing an important water source for plants, animals, and humans.

ECOSYSTEMS
(Deserts)

All over Earth, animals and plants have adapted to different living conditions caused by variations in rainfall, temperature, and wind (among other factors). One of the most challenging places to live is the desert, where water is very scarce and temperatures often alternate between blazing hot and freezing cold. But even in the desert, life can bloom. Desert plants grow deep roots to tap underground water, and tough, bristly outsides to prevent them from being eaten. Animals burrow during the day and hunt at night, when it's cooler.

GRAVITY
(Tides)

Ocean tides are caused by an ever-changing balance of gravity between Earth and the moon. The moon is much smaller than Earth, and orbits around it because of the tug of Earth's gravity. But the moon's gravity also affects Earth. As Earth rotates each day, the moon pulls at Earth's oceans, causing them to bulge out on the side closest to the moon (and the side farthest from the moon). These bulges of water are high tides. When that side of Earth rotates away from the moon, the ocean water settles back into low tide.

OCEANS
(Water Planet, Giants)

Earth's oceans cover about 71% of its surface and are home to more than a million kinds of plants and animals, which live unique and fascinating lives. Among the smallest organisms are tiny floating plants called phytoplankton—and believe it or not, they produce over half of the oxygen that we breathe! Like other plants, phytoplankton also absorb carbon dioxide (a greenhouse gas that traps heat), helping to keep Earth just the right temperature.

WATER CYCLES AND CURRENTS
(Deep Currents)

Earth's water moves in a constant cycle between land and sky: evaporating into the air, forming clouds, and raining (or snowing) back down to Earth, where it fills lakes and is absorbed by plants. Ocean water is constantly moving as well, powered by underwater currents. It heats up near the equator, where the sun is strongest, and cools down at the poles. Vast currents flow between these heated and cooled areas, creating a global "conveyer belt" that brings fresh nutrients to all parts of the ocean.

Did you know that your own body is 60% water? The water inside you is always moving, too, helping to control your body temperature. Water pumps through your blood, carrying oxygen and other nutrients. Water fills all the cells in your body, allowing them to absorb those nutrients. We evolved from sea creatures. Is it any wonder many of us feel at home in the water?

HUMAN IMPACT
(Noisy, Our Part)

Yes, Earth is big and we are small—but humans have had a huge impact on the earth. Since 1970, our population has doubled, up to over 7.6 billion people in 2020. Homes, industry, and farms for all these people have changed much of Earth's landscape and driven many species of plants and animals to extinction. Changes that make human lives easier and more productive have not always been good for the Earth. The lights of our cities and the constant noise of our machines confuse animals, disrupting their lives. The burning of fossil fuels to power our factories, homes, and cars produces air pollution that alters the climate. And chemical run-off from farms, lawns, and manufacturing degrades our water. Our desire for newer, cheaper products results in billions of tons of trash each year. We humans currently recycle only about 10% of the plastic we use. The rest of it remains in the environment forever, breaking into smaller and smaller particles. Many animals eat it, thinking it is food (and starve as a result). Tiny fragments of plastic have even been found in the water we drink. Yet there are ways that each one of us can help (see "Living with the Earth").

MESSAGES FROM THE EARTH

(Questions and Answers)

The Earth is indeed sending us messages. As the atmosphere gradually warms due to climate change, weather patterns are becoming more unpredictable. Storms are bigger and droughts are more severe. Wildfires burn out of control. Our ocean water levels are rising, swamping coastal cities. These are Earth's reminders that water, air, and soil are all precious resources, and we must treasure and protect them.

NEW SPECIES

(Mysteries)

Although we know a lot about the Earth, many mysteries remain. In 2018 alone, scientists discovered over 200 new species in overlooked or unexplored places. Scientists are also puzzling over larger questions: How exactly did life begin on Earth? How many different species are there? What life exists in the deepest parts of the ocean? How do migrating animals instinctively know where to go? Do trees really talk to one another? Are we alone in the universe? Someday, you might help solve these mysteries!

LIVING WITH THE EARTH

(Rainbow, Always at Home)

Astronauts have said that when looking down at Earth from space, they see no borders—just one planet, all connected. Everything we do on Earth has an impact upon all of us who share it. So how can we honor the Earth? By changing our everyday actions. We can:

- Reuse what we have instead of buying new products.

- Reduce our use of water and air conditioning.

- Avoid single-use plastic (like plastic cups, drinking straws, bags, and water bottles).

- Recycle as much as we can.

- Choose Earth-friendly products and cleaner sources of energy.

- Become citizen scientists, supporting scientific research by studying nature in our own backyards.

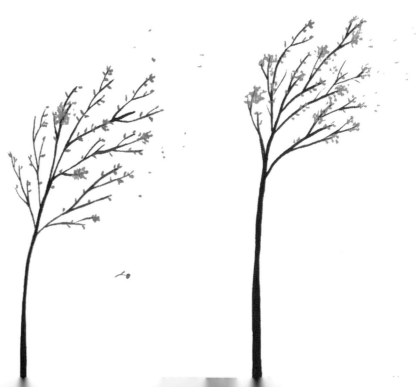

TO FIND OUT MORE, EXPLORE THE RESOURCES BELOW:

UNDERSTANDING CLIMATE CHANGE

Climate basics for kids—why our climate is changing, how it affects us, and what we can do:
c2es.org/content/climate-basics-for-kids

climatekids.nasa.gov/climate-change-meaning

More in-depth information about climate change and global warming from NASA:
climate.nasa.gov

WAYS KIDS CAN HELP

Kids' empowerment blog featuring zero waste and recycling topics:
kidsrecycle.org

Simple ways to help the planet every day, from *National Geographic*:
kids.nationalgeographic.com/explore/science/green-tips

Teacher resources and videos, from *The Nature Conservancy*:
natureworkseverywhere.org/resources

Fun ways to explore the natural world:
nationalgeographic.com/family

CITIZEN SCIENCE PROJECTS

Websites that provide ways to become a "citizen scientist" by observing and reporting on the natural world in your own backyard.

Birds: feederwatch.org

Plants: budburst.org

Pollinators: greatsunflower.org

Various: nationalgeographic.org/idea/citizen-science-projects

FOR FURTHER READING:

Bang, Molly, and Penny Chisholm. *Rivers of Sunlight: How the Sun Moves Water Around the Earth*. Illus. Molly Bang. New York: Blue Sky, 2017.

Burns, Loree Griffin. *Citizen Scientists: Be a Part of Scientific Discovery from Your Own Backyard*. New York: Square Fish, 2012.

Carson, Mary Kay. *Why Does Earth Spin? and Other Questions About Our Planet*. Illus. Peter Bull. Toronto: Sterling, 2014.

French, Jess. *What a Waste: Trash, Recycling, and Protecting Our Planet*. New York: DK Children, 2019.

Goldsmith, Mike. *Earth: the Life of a Planet*. Illus. Mark A. Garlick. London: Kingfisher, 2011.

Jeffers, Oliver. *Here We Are: Notes for Living on Planet Earth*. New York: Philomel, 2017.

Jenkins, Steve. *Earth: By the Numbers*. Boston: Houghton Mifflin Harcourt, 2019.

Portis, Antoinette. *Hey, Water!* New York: Neal Porter Books, 2019.

Sayre, April Pulley. *Thank You, Earth: A Love Letter to Our Planet*. New York: Greenwillow Books, 2018.

Stewart, Melissa. *A Place for Butterflies*. Illus. Higgins Bond. Atlanta: Peachtree, 2014.